Helpful Hints for Students and Families

Materials You Will Need:

- Pencils

- Extra paper or a notebook/journal (Everything can go in one place.)

- Colored pencils, scissors, markers, or crayons for some of the activities

Directions & Tips

- You may complete the activities in any order.

- Check off each activity as you finish it on the menu.

- Make sure an adult signs the activity menu page before you bring it back to school.

Activity Menu

	Day 1	Day 2	Day 3	Day 4	Day 5
Reading	Read for 15 minutes each day and choose one activity from your Reading Log to do.					
Writing	Kindergarten Writing Journal: My Day	My Favorite Recess Activity	My Favorite Pizza	Jump Into Writing: Write a "Car" Sentence	Kindergarten Writing Journal: Family
Math	Counting Bird Addition	Two-Dimensional Shapes	Counting to 20: Mama Bird	Number Maze 3	Finish the Pattern
Other Fun Stuff	Color the Train Back to School Sudoku Make a Match: Street Signs				

Parent/Guardian Signature: _____

Reading Log to do

1. Read a book by yourself or with a grown-up.

2. Put your name and the title of the book at the top of a new page.

3. Choose one of the ideas and write one or two sentences about your book. Remember, not all of the questions make sense for every book.

4. Don't forget to tell why or how you know, or both if you can!

How did the story end?	Who is your favorite character?	Is this book like any other book you have read? Which one?
How does the main character feel in this book?	Which words in the book were tricky?	Where does the story take place (the setting)?
What is your favorite part of the story?	What is the big problem in the story? How is it solved?	What did you learn from reading this book?
What friend or family member might like this book?	When does the story take place (the setting)?	At the end, did any characters change from how they felt at the beginning?
What is your favorite picture in the book?	What did the author want you to learn?	What surprised you in the book?

Name: _____ Date: _____

Kindergarten Writing Journal: My Day

Use the box below to draw a picture of your day. Then finish the sentences to write about your day.

First, | _____

Then, | _____

Finally, | _____

Name:_____   Date:_____

Counting Bird Addition

Count the birds to complete each addition problem. Then, trace the numbers and write your answers in the empty box.

🕊️ + 🕊️ = ☐   1 + 1 = ☐

🐣🐣 + 🐣🐣🐣 = ☐   2 + 3 = ☐

🦉🦉 + 🦉🦉 = ☐   2 + 2 = ☐

🐧🐧🐧 + 🐧 = ☐   3 + 1 = ☐

My Favorite Recess Activity

Name _____   Date _____

What is Your Favorite Recess Activity?

 slide    swing    jump rope

My favorite recess activity is _____.

Draw Your Favorite Activity

Because...
_____
_____
_____
_____

and because...
_____
_____
_____
_____

That's why I love _____.

Two-Dimensional Shapes

Trace, color, and write

Trace each shape.

square circle triangle rectangle

Color the squares blue.   Color the triangles green.
Color the circles orange.   Color the rectangles red.

Write S on all squares.   Write T on all triangles.
Write R on all rectangles.   Write C on all circles.

Name_____ Date_____

My Favorite Pizza

Izzy the Iguana loves bug pizza! Draw and write about your favorite kind of pizza. Does it have cheese? Toppings?

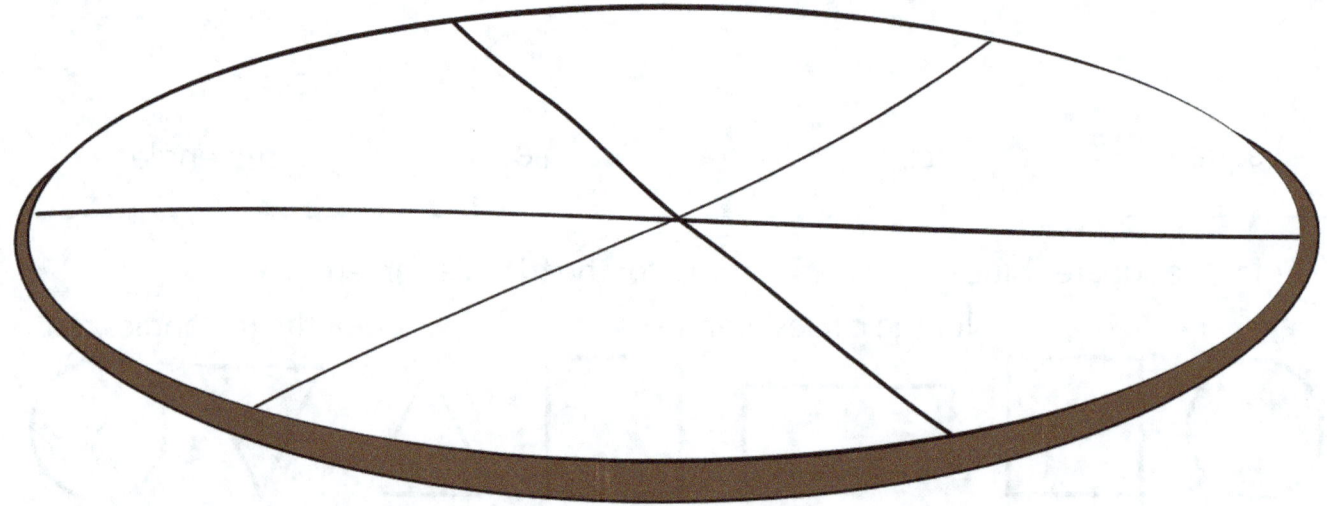

My favorite pizza is

Follow the path from 1 to 20 and help Mama Bird get to the nest.

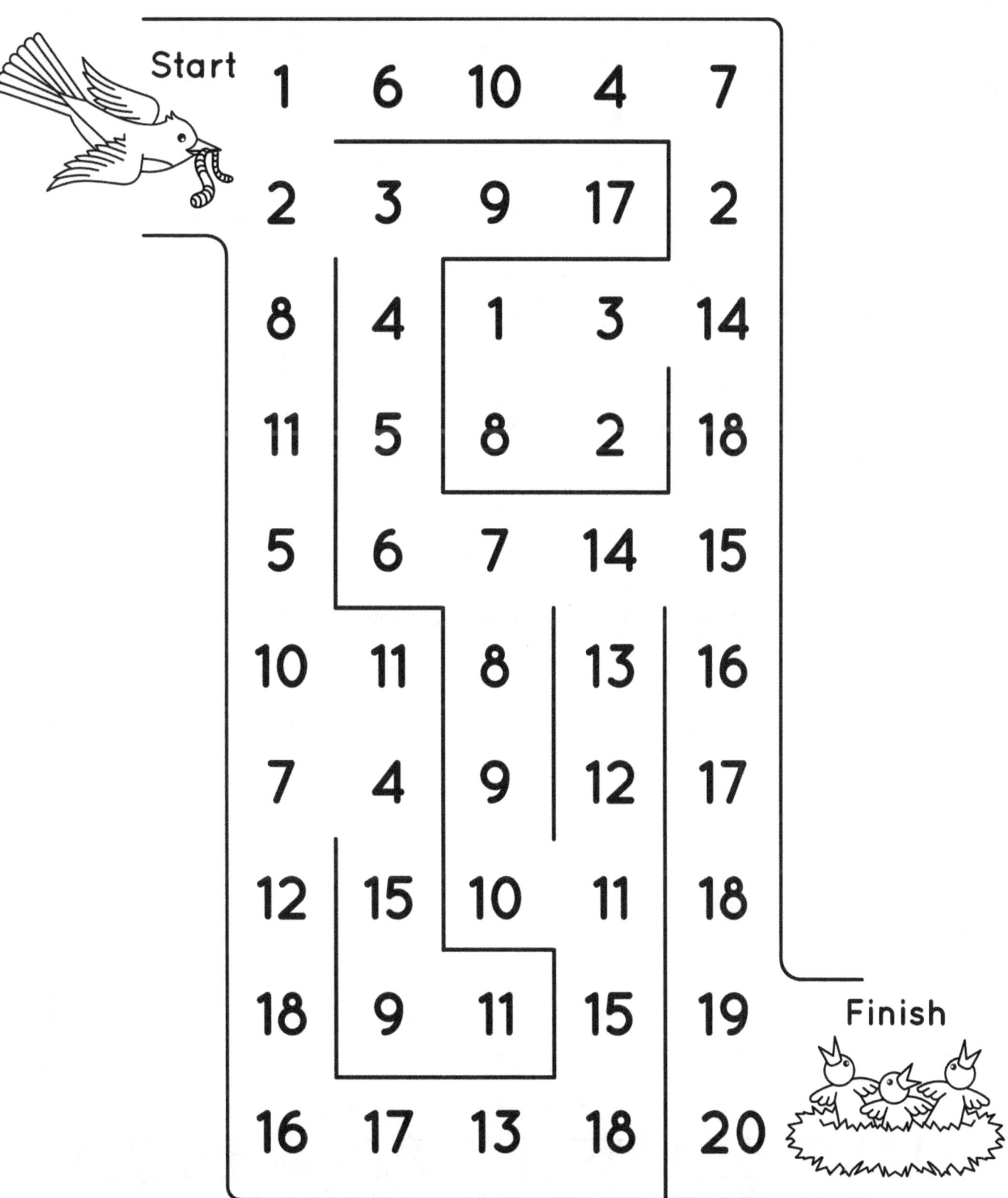

Name _____ Date _____

Writing

Trace then write the word "car" on the lines below.

Car _____

Use the word "car" in a sentence.

_____

- -

_____

- -

_____

- -

Draw a picture in the box to go with your sentence.

Follow these steps to draw your own car!

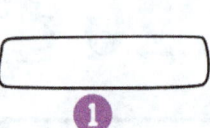 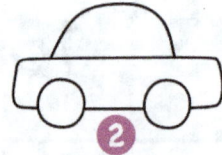  

① ② ③ ④

NUMBER MAZE 3

Can you help this rubber ducky take a bath? Draw a path from the rubber ducky to the bath tub by counting from 1 to 10 and tracing the numbers.

		8	4	6	5
		10	2	3	4
3	1	5	1	8	9
1	2	3	6	7	10
4	6	4	5		
5	2	9	2		

Name: _____ Date: _____

Kindergarten Writing Journal: Family

Use the lines below to draw a picture of the people in your family. Label the picture and use the lines to write words.

Name: _____   Date: _____

Finish the Pattern

Look at each pattern. Finish the pattern by drawing the missing shapes.

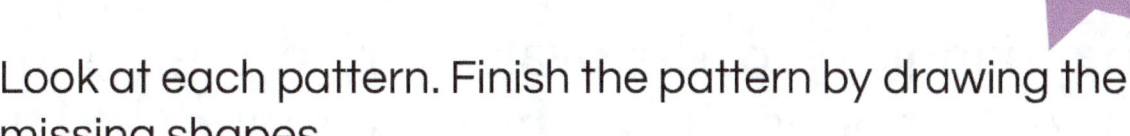

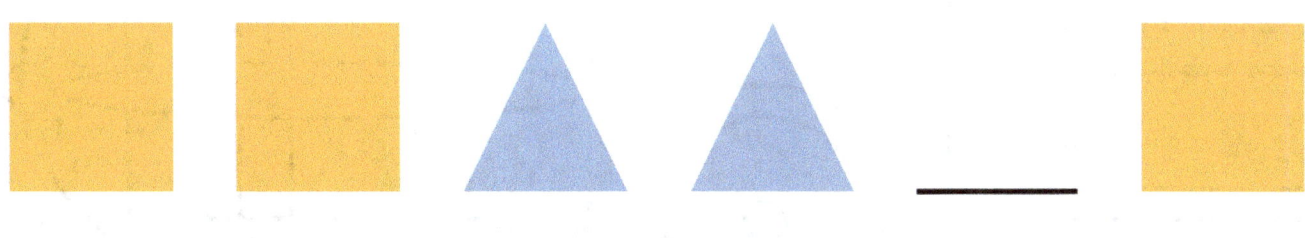

Color the Train!

Color the triangles red, the ovals orange, the squares yellow, the diamonds green, the circles blue, and the rectangles brown.

Back to School Sudoku

easy

This is a Sudoku puzzle!
To play, cut out the pictures and glue each one in the correct square. Remember: The pencil, school bus, scissors, and backpack must appear only once in each row, column, and block.

MAKE A MATCH: STREET SIGNS

Cut out the game pieces below, mix them up and place them face down on the floor. Begin the game by turning one piece over, then another. If they match, put them in a pile. If they don't match, turn both pieces over and try again. Repeat until you've made all 8 matches.

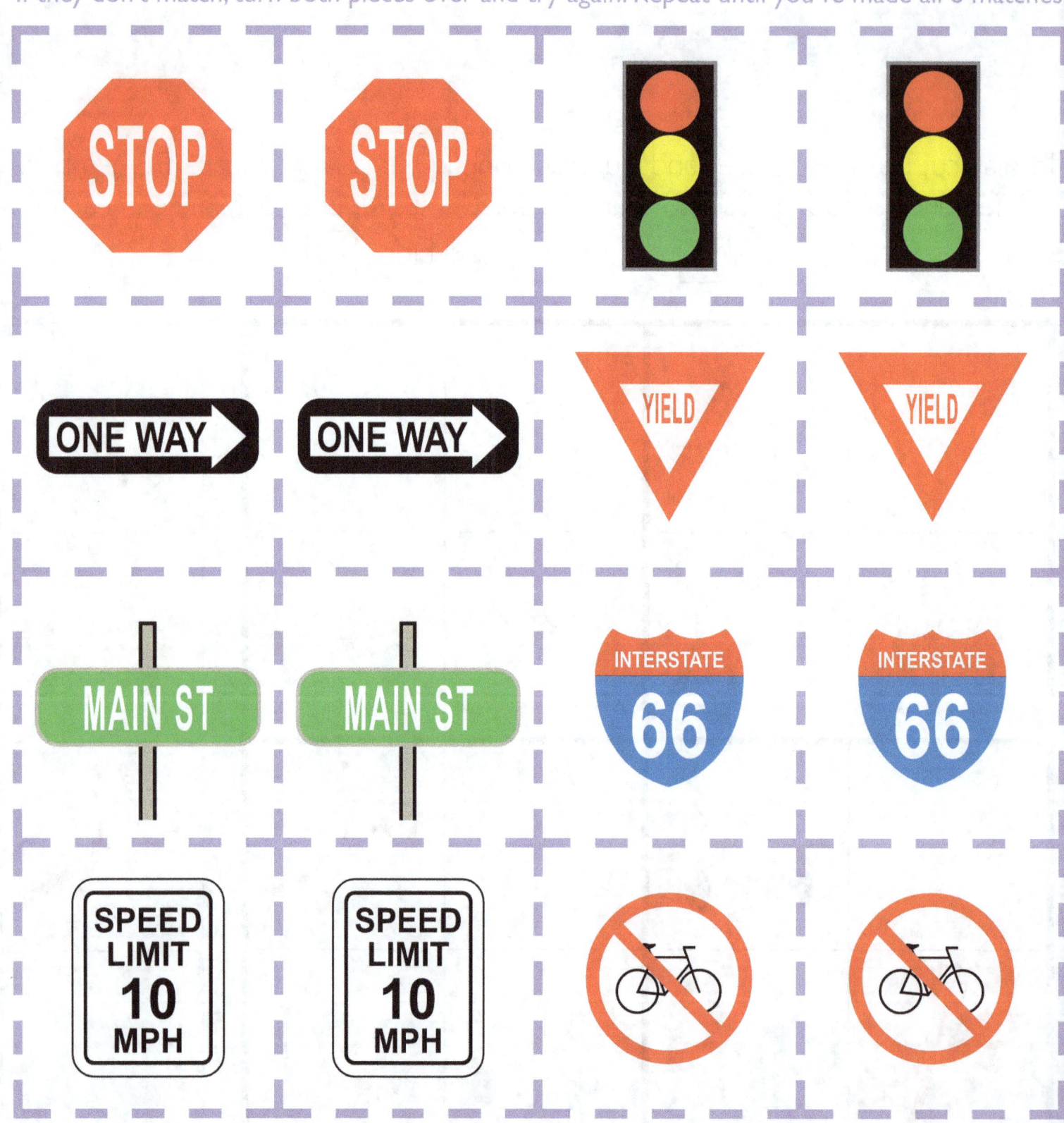

Week 1

Independent Study Packet

ANSWER KEYS

Use these answer keys to check your work!

Name: _____ Date: _____

Counting Bird Addition Answer Key

Count the birds to complete each addition problem. Then, trace the numbers and write your answers in the empty box.

🕊 + 🕊 = **2** | 1 + 1 = **2**

🐣🐣
🐣🐣 + 🐣 = **5** | 2 + 3 = **5**

🦉🦉 + 🦉🦉 = **4** | 2 + 2 = **4**

🐧🐧 + 🐧🐧 = **4** | 3 + 1 = **4**

Two-Dimensional Shapes

Trace, color and write Answer Key

Trace each shape.

 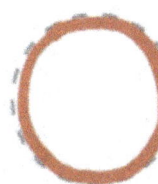  

square circle triangle rectangle

Color the squares blue. Color the triangles green.
Color the circles orange. Color the rectangles red.

Write S on all squares. Write T on all triangles.
Write R on all rectangles. Write C on all circles.

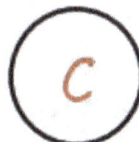      

  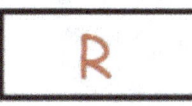    

Follow the path from 1 to 20 and help Mama Bird get to the nest. Answer Key

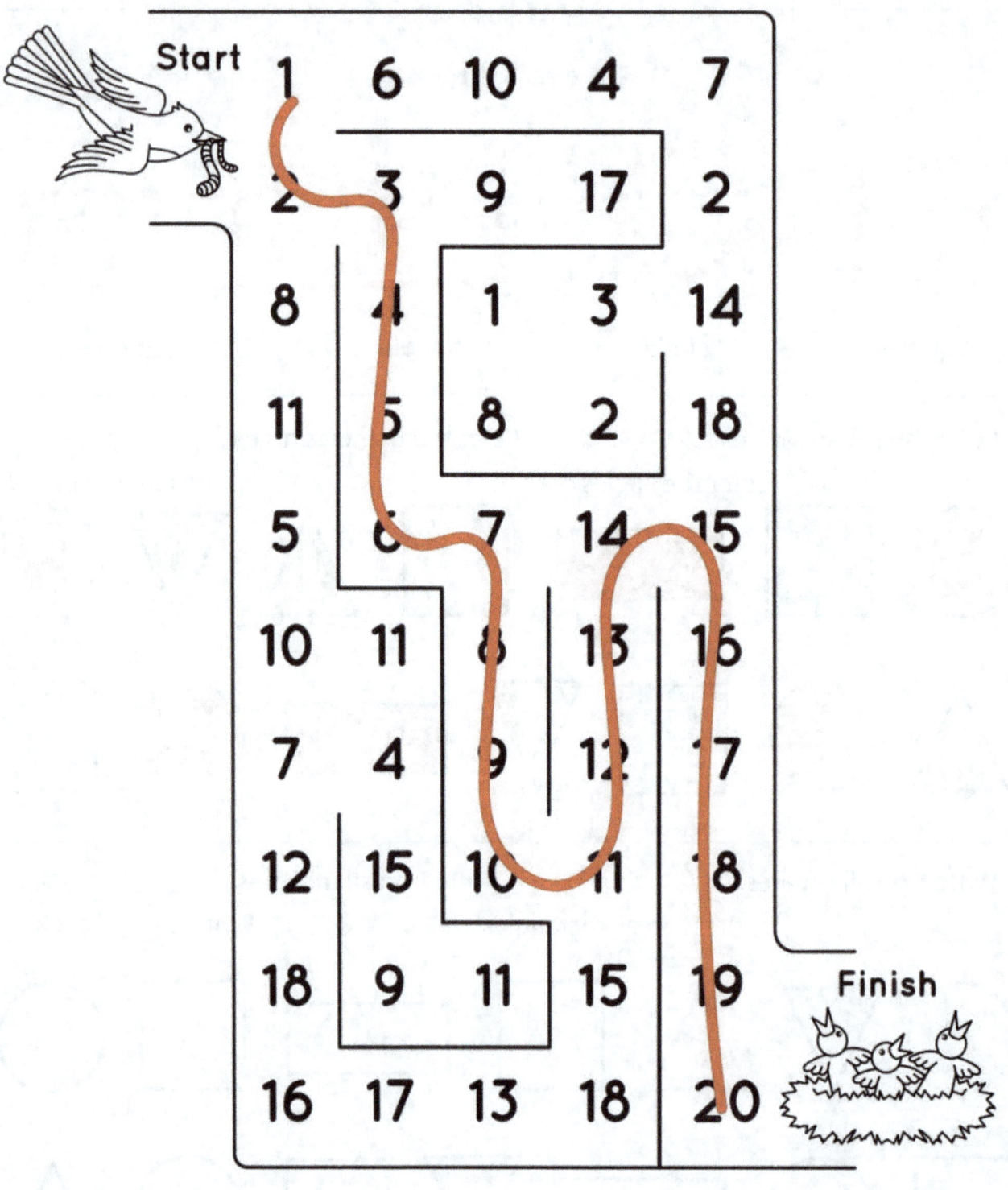

NUMBER MAZE 3

Answer Key

Can you help this rubber ducky take a bath? Draw a path from the rubber ducky to the bath tub by counting from 1 to 10 and tracing the numbers.

		8	4	6	5
		10	2	3	4
3	1	5	1	8	9
1	2	3	6	7	10
4	6	4	5		
5	2	9	2		

Name: _____   Date: _____

Finish the Pattern Answer Key

Look at each pattern. Finish the pattern by drawing the missing shapes.

Color the Train! Answer Key

Color the triangles red, the ovals orange, the squares yellow, the diamonds green, the circles blue, and the rectangles brown.

Back to School Sudoku

easy

This is a Sudoku puzzle! **Answer Key**
To play, cut out the pictures and glue each one in the correct square. Remember: The pencil, school bus, scissors, and backpack must appear only once in each row, column, and block.

Number Fun

Say the name of each number. Which letter will complete the word?
Draw a line connecting the letter to the name of each number.
Then write the letter in the blank.

2   __wo   s

4   __our   t

6   __ix   t

10 __en   f

How's the Weather?

Say the name of each picture. Which letter will complete the word? Draw a line connecting the letter to the name of each picture. Then write the letter in the blank.

Transportation

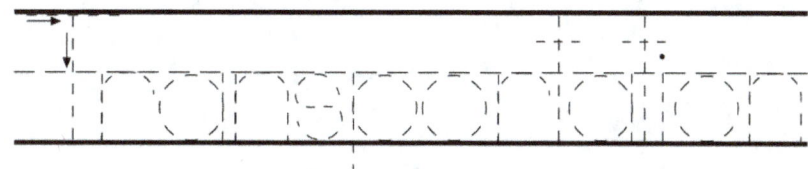

Unscramble each word to find the name of a vehicle, then write it in the space provided. When you're done, draw a line from the word to the matching picture.

peje

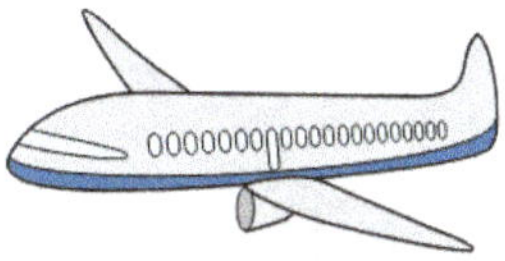

rac

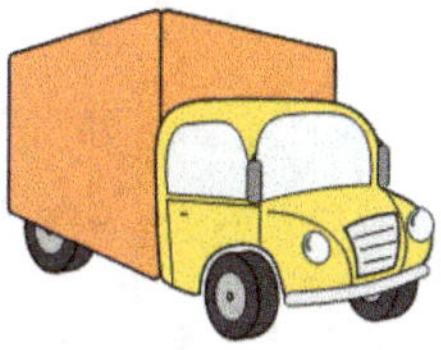

keib

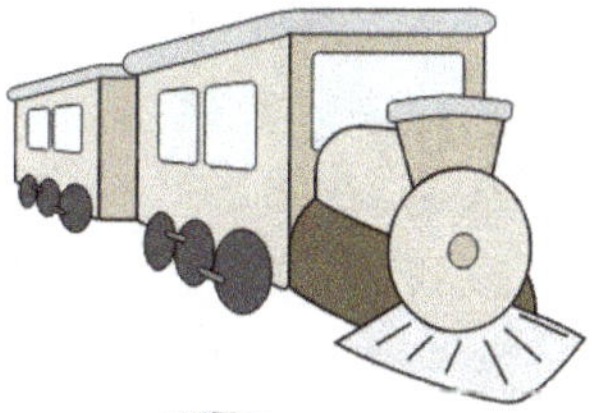

ratin

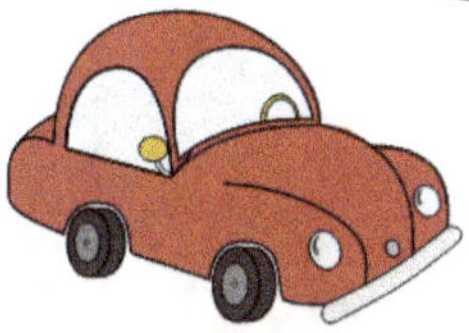

anple

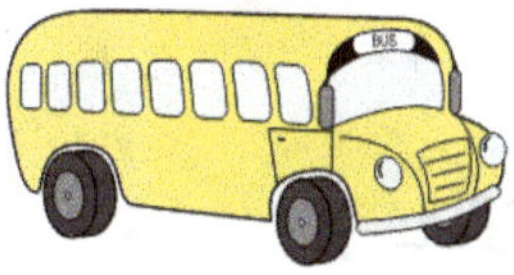

atbo

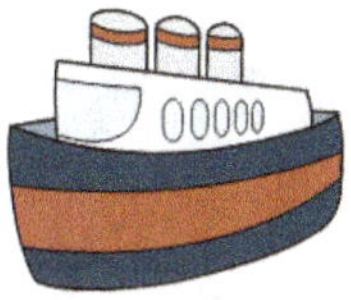

sub

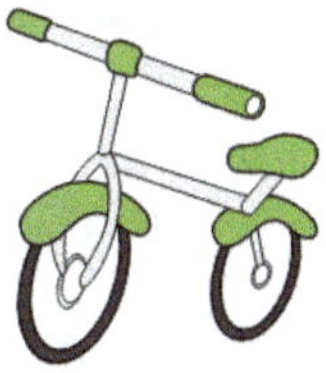

rckut

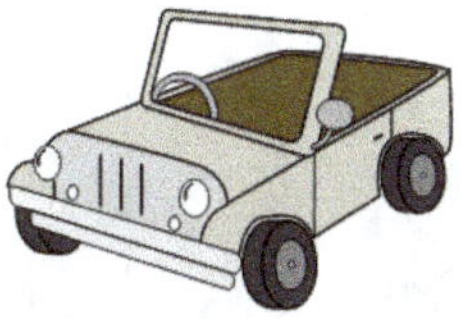

Kitchen

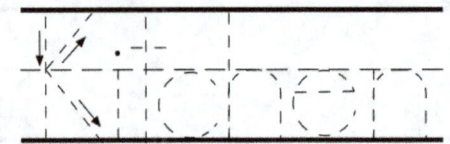

Unscramble each word to find the name of a kitchen utensil, then write it in the space provided. When you're done, draw a line from the word to the matching picture.

ugm

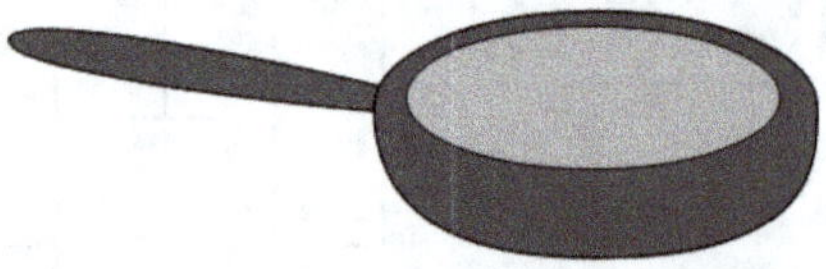

nap

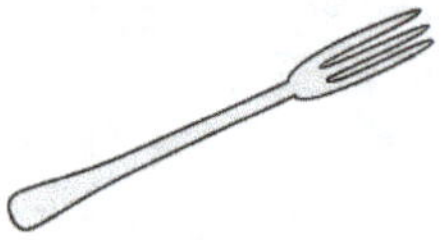

onosp

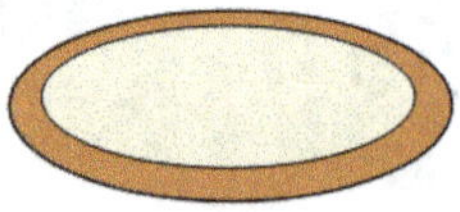

rofk

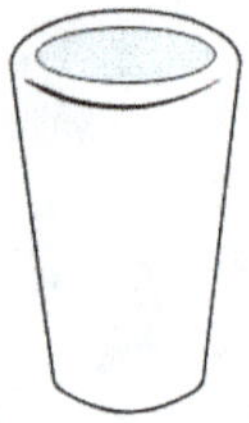

ifkne

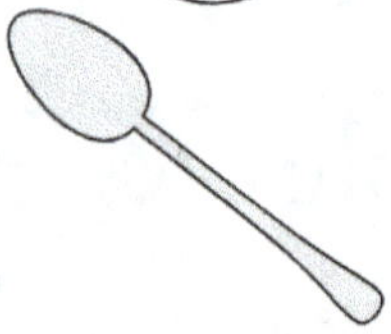

ihds

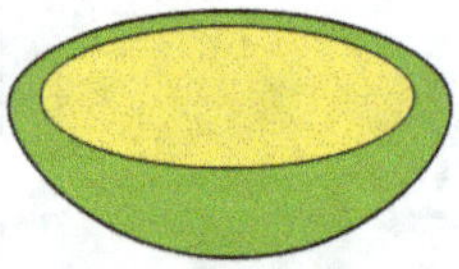

lsasg

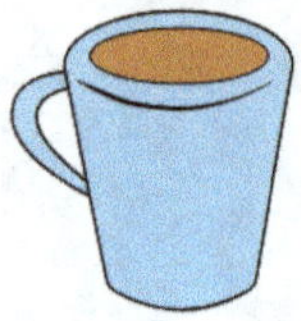

wolb

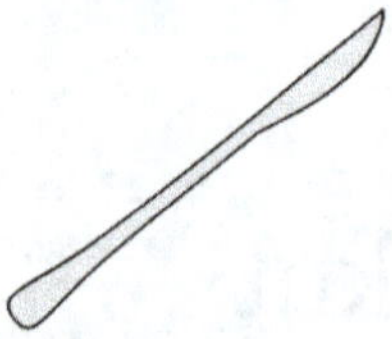

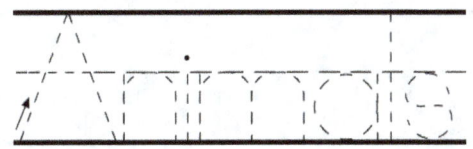

Unscramble each word to find the name of an animal, then write it in the space provided. When you're done, draw a line from the word to the matching picture.

elmu

kucd

osome

rbid

osoeg

omues

woc

ebe

Instruments

Unscramble each word to find the name of an instrument, then write it in the space provided. When you're done, draw a line from the word to the matching picture.

eltfu

artiug

inoap

rmud

pahr

onrh

pumtret

nilivo

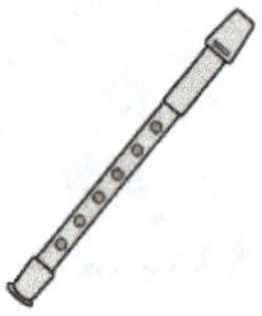

Trace And Tell

What do dogs like to eat?

Trace on the dotted lines to find out what dogs like to eat. Then trace on the letters to spell out the word and color the picture.

Trace And Tell

What do monkeys like to eat?

Trace on the dotted lines to find out what monkeys like to eat. Then trace on the letters to spell out the word and color the picture.

Learning Sight Words

Use the sight word "play" to fill in the blanks to complete each sentence

The school _____ is this weekend.

Can Tommy come over to _____?

Do you want to _____ with me?

Name the Colors

Write the name of the color of each picture using the word bank at the bottom of the page.

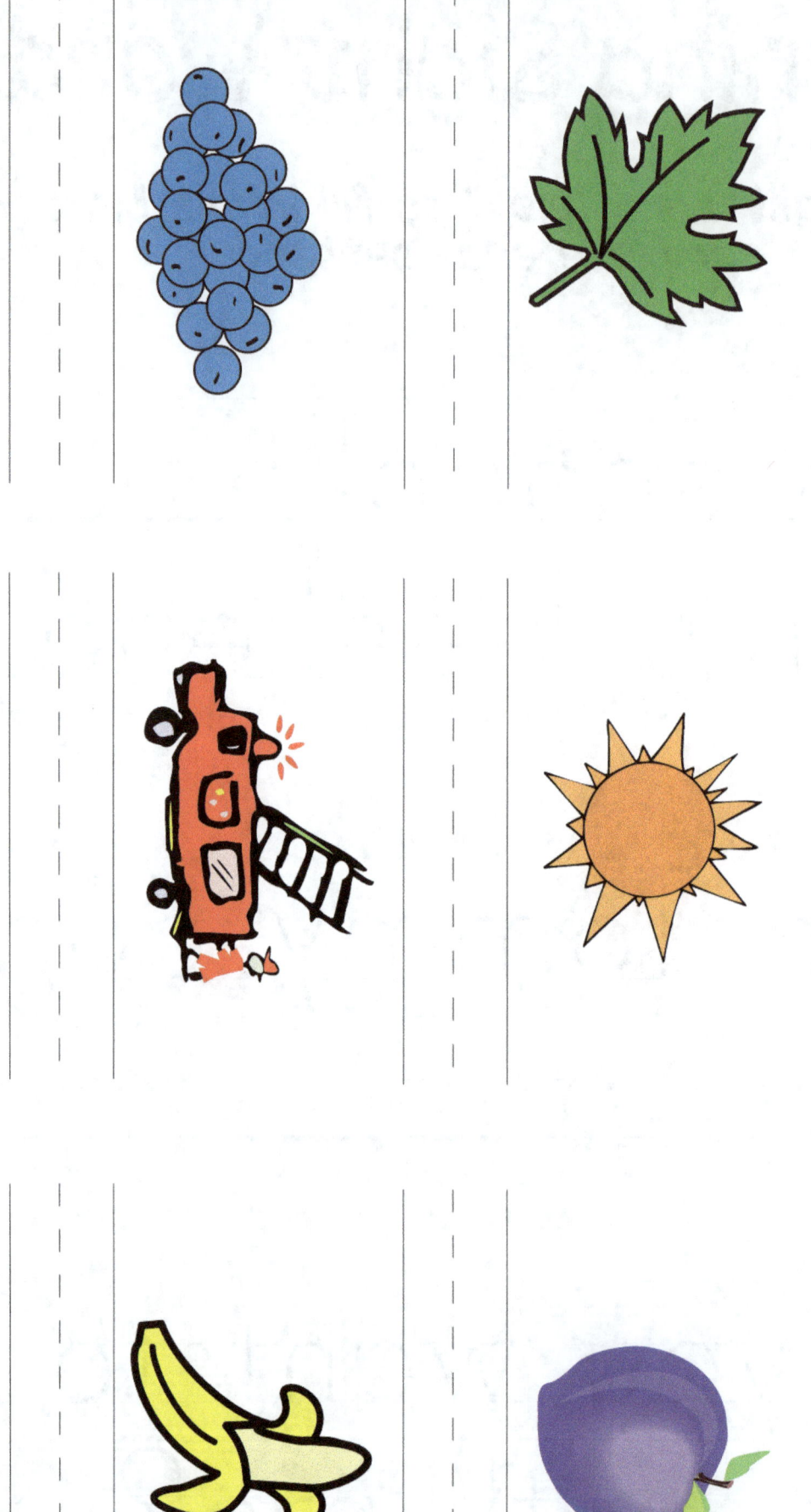

red, orange, yellow, green, blue, purple

Name the Colors

Write the name of the color of each picture using the word bank at the bottom of the page.

_ _ _ _ _ _ _

_ _ _ _ _ _ _

_ _ _ _ _ _ _

_ _ _ _ _ _ _

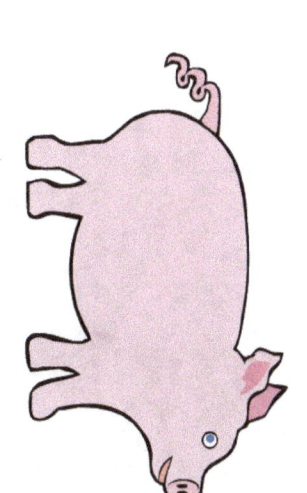

_ _ _ _ _ _ _

pink, black, brown, white, grey

All about Trees

The parts of this tree are all mixed up. Name each part correctly using the words below.

root, fruit, branch, leaf, trunk

Letter Sudoku: ABCD

easy

This is a Sudoku puzzle!
To play, fill in each blank square with the correct letter.
Remember: The letters **A**, **B**, **C**, and **D** must appear only once in each row, column, and block.

D	A	B	C
	C		A
A	B	C	D
	D		B

Kindergarten Writing — Write a Sentence

Cat

Use the word cat in a sentence.

Draw a picture in the box to go with your sentence.

① ② ③ ④

Follow these steps to draw your own cat!

Seasonal Variety — How's the Weather? POSTCARDS

Seasonal Variety — How's the Weather? POSTCARDS

Seasonal Variety — How's the Weather? POSTCARDS

Seasonal Variety — How's the Weather? POSTCARDS

Use the back of each postcard to tell a friend about what the weather is like where you live. Write about the kind of things you see this time of year: snow, blooming flowers, falling leaves, or sunny skies. When you're done, you can ask an adult to help you cut out each card and mail them!

DOG THANK YOU CARD

Color in the picture. Ask a grown-up to fold and cut out the card shape. Open the card and write something inside. Don't forget to sign your name!

IMPORTANT! Cut out the shape **after** folding on the dotted line.

Fold here

Works best printed on thicker paper!

Cut after folding!

www.ingramcontent.com/pod-product-compliance
Lightning Source LLC
Chambersburg PA
CBHW081628100526
44590CB00021B/3655